I'LL HAVE THE LAW ON YOU

The Selected Letters of John Fytit

Paul Brennan

Author of "101 Reasons to Kill All the Lawyers - that part which Laws or Lawyers can Cause or Cure"

A  Production

First edition published in 2015.

Published by Brief Books, Mooloolaba, Queensland Australia 4557.

National Library of Australia Cataloguing-in-Publication entry.

Creator: Brennan, Paul, 1954- author.

Title: I'll Have The Law On You: The Selected Letters of John Fytit / Paul Brennan.

ISBN: 9780987489425 (paperback)

Subjects: Law--Humor.
          Legal correspondence.
          Legal aid.
          Legal consultants.

Dewey Number: 340

Author: Brennan, Paul (1954 -)

Edited and proofed by Kathleen Brennan.

This work is copyright. Apart from any use as permitted under the Copyright Act 1968, no part may be reproduced, copied, scanned, stored in a retrieval system, recorded or transmitted in any form or by any means without the prior written permission of the publisher.

Copyright © 2015.

Brief Books, PO Box 27, Mooloolaba, Queensland Australia 4557.
BN22069914   ABN 60 583 357 067. Phone: 617 5438 8199
www.lawanddisorder.com.au
For other publications by the author see http://www.amazon.com/Paul-Brennan/e/B001KMQFEC

The right of Paul Brennan to be identified as the author of this work has been asserted by him under the Copyright Amendment (Moral Rights) Act 2000.

Cover design by Luke Perkins Graphics.

Graphics by Joselito Mahilum.

Layout, typesetting and print design by Toni Esser.

Printed by Createspace.

To my wife, Diane.

Contents

Preface		5
PART 1	The Seven Traits Of Lawyers	6
PART 2	Advice To Lawyers	15
PART 3	Complaints Against Legal Institutions And Traditions	25
PART 4	Career Advice And Self-Help	31
PART 5	Couples Complaining About Their Adult Children And Each Other	42
PART 6	Adult Children Concerned About Their Inheritance Being Mismanaged	54
PART 7	Advice On Issues Raised By People With Nothing Better To Do	63
PART 8	General Irritations Of Life	77
Conclusion		89

PREFACE

My apologies to the many judges, prosecutors, politicians, ombudsmen and lawyers who have benefited from Fytit's advice but whose letters do not appear here.

PART 1

THE SEVEN TRAITS OF LAWYERS

Many of the letters sent to Fytit's column were barely concealed complaints against lawyers. Certain common traits can be identified ranging from amusing eccentricities such as scruffiness, to darker personality defects such as procrastination.

I have tried where possible to disguise the identity of the lawyers involved who may be familiar to the reader.

Trait 1: Scruffiness

Dear John,

My lawyer is so scruffy that I am ashamed to be seen with him in court. I am worried that the other lawyers look down on him. What can I do to make him more presentable?

I for one, believe that there is no excuse, even for inept lawyers, not to look their best when in the company of clients. It is the least they can do. Standard of dress is something that judges look for, in addition to legal argument. I have seen cases lost for the want of a trouser press.

Tell him that you do not expect Beau Brummel, but to get a grip.

Trait 2: Procrastination

Dear John,

Is there any way that I can speed up my lawyer? The only thing that he did promptly during the present transaction was to go on vacation half way through it.

I assume that we are dealing with a delay of months rather than years or, in some cases, decades. Generally, except in the case of legal issues arising at 4.50pm on a Friday afternoon, a lawyer's pace does not alter. They tend to show their form early on, and like racehorses, it is best to get rid of the back markers.

It can be a recognized disorder, Procrastinating Attorney Inactivity Nuisance Syndrome ("PAINS"). Over the years, a Procrastinating Attorney ("PA") develops coping mechanisms that can make it hard to spot. He will insist on written communications only, his being intermittent. When pressed he will claim that he was waiting for instructions from his client which may be a surprise to that client. He will call for careful consideration of legal issues while doing little or nothing himself.

I'll Have the Law on You

If you finally decide to change lawyers, the PA will insist on being paid. To avoid argument and further delay, seek donations from the other party and lawyer to the transaction. They may be more than willing to contribute as they have suffered too.

Alternatively, turn to one of the many associations and organisations who are willing to help. Here is an extract from one such organisation's website:

- Are you afraid to upset your lawyer for fear he will delay even more?

- Do you make threats such as, "If you don't get a move on, I'll leave you"?

- Do you have money problems because of your lawyer's delay?

- Do you tell lies to cover up for your lawyer?

- Do you think that if your lawyer stopped delaying, your other problems would be solved?

If you have answered "yes" to any of these questions, Clients' Anonymous ("C-Anon") could help you.

Part 1

How will C-Anon help me?

In C-Anon you will meet others who share your frustration. It has expanded not only to include clients but other lawyers, partners, spouses, employees, judges and others who have been affected by the delay of a PA.

How does a PA affect others?

PAINS is a progressive disorder and only the PA can stop the delay. However, they never seem to get round to it.

We focus on them, we try to control their delay and do their work for them. We take on the blame and guilt that really belongs to the PA.

I hope that this helps.

Trait 3: Reticence in Court

Dear John,

I have just changed lawyers and, although satisfied with my choice, my wife tells me that the man down the road says my new lawyer is a pussycat in court.

How can I know if I have made the right choice? Any advice he gives me will now be devalued due to this slur against him. Should I change again?

I'll Have the Law on You

Stop changing lawyers all the time. It doesn't do any good. Tell your lawyer that the man down the road said that he was a pussycat in court. If he successfully sues the pants off this man for defamation, then you not only have the satisfaction of proving your wife wrong but you get to see him in action in court. If your wife gossips, the lawyer may sue her too. Serves her right.

Trait 4: Failure to Recognise a Client

Dear John,

My lawyer never recognises me, it is as if he is meeting a stranger each time. He has been my lawyer for 10 years and although I do not expect a red carpet, I would like him to know who I am. Is this absentmindedness or arrogance?

At your next appointment, ask your lawyer for money. Your lawyer will never forget you again. This not only works with lawyers but accountants. Although with accountants, watch out for seizures and any other adverse medical reaction that could lead to a claim. It does not work with bankers who treat requests for money

Part 1

with indifference or mild amusement, although missed repayments work pretty well.

If it were arrogance, your lawyer would not see you at all and leave it to his secretary.

I am sure your own lawyer would be mortified by your concern, as I would be if you were one of my clients. Which you are not, are you?

Trait 5: Not Listening

Dear John,

My lawyer never really listens to me. What can I do?

If they did teach listening at Law School, I certainly don't remember it.

In any event, young lawyers have the unique ability to know what a person's legal problem is before they sit down, and therefore, do not need to listen.

It's true that older lawyers do find listening tiresome. However, except for the occasional

HAPPY BIRTHDAY AT THE MAGISTRATES COURT

I'll Have the Law on You

client who comes in for a will and ends up divorced, it has worked pretty well over the centuries. Lawyers with extreme hearing problems are, of course, quickly appointed magistrates.

On the positive side, if lawyers took time to listen, your legal bills would go up and then where would we be?

Trait 6: Arrogance

Dear John,

My lawyer is full of himself. He is not so bad when I see him on his own in his office. Yet, when we are at meetings with others, especially lawyers, he becomes quite unbearable. Should I tell him?

Some lawyers do have a lot to feel smug about. It is just that most of them are exceptionally good at hiding it.

I find lawyers with a slightly regal presence, male or female, can add to the occasion of any meeting. If you have seen Lady Catherine de Bourgh in the BBC production of Pride and Prejudice, you will know the sort of thing I mean.

Part 1

However, lawyers with a pained expression and whiny tone are hard to bear. When I get to that stage, I intend to seek help.

You can tell your lawyer, but it sounds as if he may have developed Attention Pained Rectal Attorney Trauma ("APRAT") for which the most effective course is an intervention by his own partners. Some firms set aside every Monday for such interventions so it may just be a matter of booking him in.

Trait 7: Ignoring Others Due to Claims of Pressure of Work

Dear John,

I recently asked my lawyer to sue someone and almost immediately regretted it. He always seems so busy. I hate bothering him. Even money does not seem to make him any happier.

How should I get his attention?

All lawyers are busy until they learn the principles of good practice management.

I give priority to clients who have some sort of

run in with say, another motorist or their bank, and are content to be told that they have a great case but cannot afford to sue. This is a comparatively cheap and quick service. For many it brings closure so that they can get on with their lives.

In the more involved case, it is necessary to spend many hours collating documents and preparing a stinging and authoritative letter to the offending party. This can be tiring but very rewarding for the client. Often, I decide not to send the letter out. I do not tell the client that I have not sent it. The client has the satisfaction of savaging their enemy without the upset of a shot being fired in return. If I receive an unpleasant letter from the other side, I often do not pass it on to the client. Over the years, I have found that this keeps everybody happy.

If my client happens to find out that the letter has not been received by their enemy, they blame and even consider suing the Post Office. However, they usually accept my advice that although they have an excellent case, it is not wise to open up a second front and they cannot afford it anyway.

I imagine the lawyer on the other side does the same.

Of course, if my practice does slow down, I dig up a few of these old letters and send them off. This helps to moderate the case flow in my office. Therefore, unlike your lawyer, I have time to take instructions from my clients and be ready to deal with new matters as they arise.

PART 2

ADVICE TO LAWYERS

Many lawyers who at first referred their more challenging clients to Fytit, increasingly turned to him for advice themselves.

Charity and Lawyers

Dear John,

I have heard that lawyers will be required to undertake 10 charitable hours a year under the soon to be introduced Charitable Legal Endeavours' (CLE) points scheme. While previous charitable acts will be taken into account, my last one was in 1997, and I did not even win the raffle.

Is this not just another fad foisted on the legal profession, like mediation and suspended sentences?

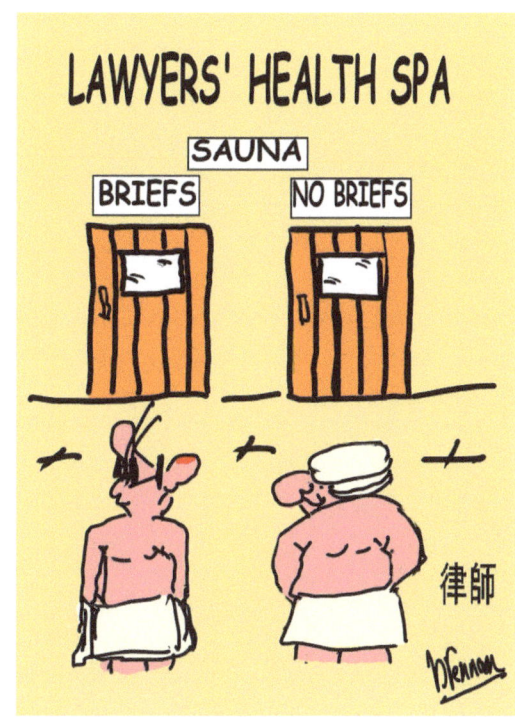

Many legal practitioners will not have any difficulty as CLEs are to include hours spent talking clients out of litigation; a daily occurrence with some clients.

I understand that the management of some larger firms insisted on a Charitable Emissions Trading Scheme (CETS) so that extra CLEs could be purchased from smaller firms and overseas to fulfil the targets of their associate lawyers to avoid any distraction from their work. Therefore, sale of CLEs may prove fruitful for smaller firms although the extra paperwork could be burdensome.

Charity seems to start with expensive clothes and unrelated strenuous activity. Mother Teresa would not get a look in these days. The other day I saw a flyer for a fund raising walk for orphans that said, "Bring the Family".

My approach to charity is that it is good for the soul. If anyone finds out about your charitable deeds, it does not count. Of course, without a marketing department it has been tricky over the years to let clients and others know how discrete and humble I am about this. However, with the right receptionist, I have managed.

Note: *Lawyers undertake Continuing Legal Education (CLE) points each year that are regarded of limited use as the younger and older lawyers know everything already.*

Part 2

Modern Partnership

Dear John,

I chose my partners at a time when "partner" meant "business partner". We all knew exactly where we stood. Now, the situation is regrettably confused.

As the use of the word "partner" expanded to suggest romantic attachment, many single business partners hoped that this would be the solution to their lonely lives, especially the ugly ones. It was subtle at first, just hints that there was something more than a business relationship with the use of words such as "darling" or "love" at the end of a sentence. Yet, soon it became, "Where were you last night?", "You never listen to me" and even "Where are my slippers?". Many partners could not stand it, and stormed out slamming the door.

THE PROPOSAL

Such was the concern in legal circles that lawyers were permitted to incorporate. We were immediately relieved that we no longer had to use the word "firm". It seemed to have gone the same way as the word "member".

I'll Have the Law on You

It was a useful reminder to us that words regarded as perfectly innocent before the war, were now a minefield. We immediately embarked on a review of our precedents, deleting references to words and phrases that could cause offence such as briefs, discharge, hung jury, motion, bond, age and restraint.

This is not to criticise those lawyers who have decided to remain in traditional partnerships. For the first time, many have been able to discuss their true feelings. Late nights at the office instead of going home to spouses were not quite what they seemed after all.

The Awardless

Dear John,

As much as I try, why does everybody win business awards except me?

Such is the proliferation of award ceremonies that I know of lawyers who are more decorated than Audie Murphy*. Even though they readily admit that it is not a reflection of their abilities, there is increasing pressure on we the "Awardless". It has even been suggested by one client that I merge with a serial Awardee to "fill the empty shelves in my reception".

I have never openly sought any recognition or praise for my work, which my wife says is probably just as well. However, my principled non-participation is now characterised as "Award Denying".

My advice is to join one of the many organisations offering awards and create your own category. For instance, an award for sober librarians or humble senior partners would certainly limit the field

In awards, as in life, 85% success is turning up. But it is possible to achieve a further 15% by changing the rules.

*The most decorated soldier of WWII who was still receiving awards in 2013 (30 years after his death).

The Internet and The Art of War

Dear John,

Now because of the internet, the first interview with a client can be like a tutorial on the subject of their legal issue. I find it very enlightening, but wish to return to the days when I gave insightful

comments rather than just listening attentively and looking it up online later.

I have known clients to painstakingly research the law on the internet only to find it has changed by the time that they get to my office. After spending hours trawling the internet, I believe clients have a better understanding of what we lawyers have had to put up with. They are relieved when I refuse to trot out the usual legal claptrap and instead focus on their issue.

I seldom use law at all but rely on *The Art of War* by Sun Tzu, a warfare manual written 2,500 years ago. It is a sort of Quentin Tarantino version of *Don't Sweat the Small Stuff*.

The Art of War is extremely effective in planning strategies. Combine its authority with the benefit of hindsight, and you will once again find yourself offering sage, insightful comments to appreciative clients.

What client would not like to be advised by their new lawyer that their previous lawyer had a) disastrously and expensively laid a prolonged siege rather than rushing forward to secure a quick victory, or alternatively b) had rushed forward rather than adopting safer ground until the time was right?

I first started to use *The Art of War* to convince trainee lawyers that everything was their fault. Previously, any discussion with them involving law always left me feeling that I was to blame.

Once you are known as an *Art of War* practitioner, other lawyers may no longer feel smug at your inaction as appearing to do nothing is the ultimate deception. You will feel a general euphoria that however bad things may appear, a brilliant, unfathomable plan is at work and will come to you eventually.

Part 2

At thirteen chapters, The Art of War is a far easier read than the entire common law, and you will be pleased to know that there was no Latin in Ancient China.

Online Justice

Dear John

I understand that there is a big push worldwide to move courts online to increase efficiency and reduce cost. Will this really help?

Although we should keep certain traditions such as having everything in triplicate, many welcome law-online as an opportunity for reform.

Here are five proposals:

1. There is no need to have a judge at every court. In the eleventh century, itinerant judges went from town to town on particular circuits dispensing the King's justice as required. Judges could be kept at a central location called a "Home" and sent to courts on request. How often would that be? Well, according to focus groups - never.

2. *Already in our courts, oral submissions have for the most part been replaced with written submissions. Would it not be more efficient to have an online questionnaire with a choice of four answers "Yes", "No", "It all depends" or "I don't know"?*

3. *Legal service consumers who have long complained about the performance and appearance of their lawyers should have a choice between standard lawyers and muscle bulging digitized virtual lawyers equipped with the type of weaponry available in any computer game.*

4. *Prison sentences and other old fashioned penalties could be replaced with virtual punishment. For instance, virtual tagging preventing offenders from going on Facebook. Community service could be served in Second Life.*

5. *I have long thought that a jury of twelve is far too small. In ancient Athens juries consisted of five hundred citizens. We could easily outdo this by using Twitter. If submissions were only 140 characters, cases could be over in minutes.*

I do not agree with those who wish to replace familiar terms such as "plaintiffs" and "defendants" with something less confrontational such as "survivors". However, litigants should be allowed to choose their own court persona to protect their privacy and spice up the court lists.

How much saving could such reforms achieve? Well, if Instagram managed thirty million subscribers with thirteen staff I think we can do better than that.

Part 2

"No Frills" Courts

Dear John

Sturdy docks and wooden benches have been replaced by plastic chairs and flimsy furnishings in our courtrooms in a "No Frills" initiative. Is this not an affront to the dignity of the judicial process?

There may be some room for a "No Frills" judiciary, for instance, cutbacks on judges' lodgings, but the courtroom is the showcase of our entire judicial system.

Airlines vary their service offering based on the quality of the passengers. There is a natural legal pecking order that would lend itself to this approach in our courtrooms. For instance, senior members of the profession should have First Class seating especially for long haul trials. At tense moments,

23

oxygen masks could drop down. For emergencies, there could be dinner jackets underneath the seats.

We would all gain from sick bags being available especially during the submissions of certain well-meaning advocates.

After lunch, lights could be dimmed, and anyone wishing to pay attention could use their reading lights.

Once we have the right seating, there will be no need to go to the canteen for morning tea. It could be brought in by the ushers thereby increasing efficiency.

Bathroom breaks have always been an issue. But a light saying "remain seated" operated by the judge could be usefully combined with loudspeaker announcements throughout the courthouse to ensure we did not miss anything.

Young lawyers would from time to time be upgraded from economy seating.

I am not in favour of earphones, movies and magazines, but these should be optional in the public gallery. Such options would be far more effective in achieving a dignified silence than the cold stares of police and ushers.

Add a court miles scheme and experiments with massage and our courts would once again become the envy of the legal world.

PART 3

COMPLAINTS AGAINST LEGAL INSTITUTIONS AND TRADITIONS

Ombudsmen

In the early years, Fytit's outbursts against Ombudsmen were widely reported but probably no more than professional jealousy on his part. Ombudsmen found Fytit's approach amusing but lacking bureaucratic rigour. It was only when Scandinavian governments started to bypass Ombudsmen and refer matters directly to Fytit that Ombudsmen resolved to act. We are not sure what happened after that.

A COMPELLING STORY UNTIL YOU REALIZE THAT THE FIRE BREATHING DRAGON WAS HIS WIFE

I'll Have the Law on You

Front Rank File

Dear John,

I brought my complaint to the attention of the Ombudsman but nothing much happened. Is there any particular approach to the Ombudsman that you would recommend?

If you have seen the film Zulu you will know what it is like to be in a government Ombudsman's office, daily risking being overrun by crazed complainants fresh from battle.

The Ombudsman's office is not allowed to use the Martini-Henry rifle and fire by rank manoeuvre, as satisfying as this may sound. However, the Ombudsman's terms of reference can be drawn so narrowly that over 75% of complaints can be opened, found to be outside the terms of reference, and closed within a matter of a few days of receipt. Unlike Zulu warriors, complainants receive a two-page, admittedly standard letter of rejection. Despite this, a customer satisfaction survey remains just as imprudent today as it was in 1879.

With the decks cleared, the Ombudsman can assess the merit of the remaining complaints and investigate appropriately. Yet, after the carnage of repelling the initial onslaught, certain government Ombudsmen can feel understandably quite worn out. They can find it hard to resist having a quick roll call and then swiftly finishing off the surviving complaints with a bureaucratic cats lick accompanied by another two-page letter.

As in so many conflicts, an Ombudsman's lack of achievement can be portrayed as a victory. Glossy brochures report a courageous, fearless dedication to duty with occasional salutes by vanquished but appreciative complainants. They contain detailed statistics proudly declaring file closures.

Shouldn't the complainants complain about this treatment? Yes, but who would believe them?

Legal Receptionists

Fytit explained not only the plight of the legal receptionist but the difficulty lawyers encountered answering the telephone.

Legal Greetings

Dear John,

My lawyer has erected a sign by the front door of his law firm saying "Welcome". Do you think that this applies to all his clients, or will he require some of us to go around the back?

I do not think a lawyer is behind this, it is more likely some brash young marketer.

I am all for throwing out the threadbare carpets but a sign saying "Welcome" raises dangerously unrealistic

expectations.

Having said this, law firms should not foster an impression of hostility. This is one of the reasons why many small law firms have removed their receptionists.

In the 1990s, law firm receptions were as busy as those of doctors. However, with the advent of email, fewer clients attended personally for interviews and due to isolation, many receptionists turned to drink. Greetings to clients, which overnight turned from stern to welcoming and even jolly, often became morose by late afternoon.

To counter this, receptionists designed higher reception desks to hide the bottles, ear pieces were employed to explain the occasional muttering and they remained seated to avoid collapse or in some cases, unseemly dancing.

Clients became used to peering over high reception desks to see the receptionist on the telephone looking into the distance, absentmindedly mumbling.

But eventually receptionists were taken into the back office, dried out and rehabilitated. Many have gone on to achieve successful careers in airport security.

Recently, a conveyancing lawyer was persuaded by his marketing

Part 3

manager to put up a sign outside his office that read, "Prepare to be amazed and astounded". His wife quickly took it down.

Holding Legal Receptionists, the Do's and Don'ts

Dear John,

Every time I call my lawyer I am put on-hold, sometimes for up to 20 minutes. It seems to me that lawyers should do more to organize their time.

If I may correct you slightly, it is not the lawyer who puts you on-hold, it is the legal receptionist over whom lawyers often have little control.

Facilitating client holding is a significant part of a legal receptionist's duties. It allows them time to whizz around all the other clients who they have on-hold asking, "Do you wish to hold?" They have been trained not to wait for a reply.

Lawyers over the centuries have tried all sorts of ways to improve client communication, the telephone being one of them. Nevertheless, even modern innovations such

29

as voicemail, email and direct lines have caused lawyers to have less time to deal with client telephone calls.

For lawyers, on-hold messaging has been a particular issue. Messages such as "Your call is important to us" have only served to antagonize clients. Lawyers have tried to make their on-hold messages a promotion for the law firm's expertise and dedication. Yet, after a number of caller suicides, such practices have, for the most part, been abandoned. On-hold legal education has been so successful, that clients too often have received the answer to their question and hung up.

Clients may need to accept being placed on-hold as part of the legal process. After all, it is one of the few free/pro bono services that lawyers provide. Theoretically, a full hour on-hold results in significant saving.

Anyway, many clients avoid speaking to their lawyer and prefer being on-hold.

PART 4

CAREER ADVICE AND SELF-HELP

Fytit used the law as a vehicle to give hope.

Life Going Nowhere?

Dear John,

My life is going nowhere. Do I have a claim?

It is only when Life Going Nowhere (LGN) Non-Activists become radicalised that they discover that it is not their fault after all. After years of self-blame, they are ready to identify and denounce those who are really responsible e.g. parents, government departments, ex-girlfriends etc.

My advice is to choose one or more abusers,

and if you are wrong you can always change later. Your therapist can assist you through this process and help to apply an appropriate label such as LGN Abuse.

Although a lone voice can generate some sympathy, to mount a legal claim you will need to encourage others to join you. With a subject such as LGN you should have no trouble, I feel like joining you myself.

Your motive must remain selfless. It is best to describe fellow sufferers as 'Survivors' which suggests overcoming adversity rather than malingering. The Survivors' mission should be to assist other Survivors and prevent their children (especially teenagers) from becoming victims. Remind them to remain humourless and easily offended at all times.

You will need a website, a trademark, t-shirts, posters, ribbons, social media consultants but most of all, a generous travel allowance to organise the World LGN Abuse Summit. The prospect of foreign travel possibly in Bali should secure the support of family and friends who may have been sceptical up to that point.

Although the lawyers at the Legal Aid Department may empathise with you, legal aid is unlikely to be available initially. Therefore, it will be necessary to raise money for legal fees and other expenses.

It is important not to beg. Offer sponsorship, membership (platinum, gold, silver) and seek celebrity endorsement. There will be those who refuse to give. Rather than listing the people who give you money, list the people who do not.

Finally, find an LGN lawyer (there is no shortage) and select a jurisdiction with imagination, such as America's state courts.

Part 4

Prosecutors

Dear John,

With crime rates falling, prosecutors have turned to their back catalogue of offences committed by ageing celebrities and others. However, with memories lapsing and witnesses dying, the evidence in such cases can be questionable or lost in time.

Should we just wait and hope that crime picks up, press on and take what we can get, or get out now?

There is no patron saint of hopeless cases, but there are many examples of prosecutors pulling some very unlikely convictions out of the hat.

For instance, during the Napoleonic Wars a ship's pet monkey was shipwrecked on a beach in the North of England. The locals captured the monkey, mistakenly believing it to be a French spy as it was dressed in military uniform.

The monkey was interrogated, tried, found guilty and hung.

I'll Have the Law on You

In that case, the burden would have been on the prosecutor to prove beyond reasonable doubt that the monkey had an intention to spy, no easy task.

Let us not forget the defence lawyer's task of taking clear instructions long before the advent of dedicated animal rights' lawyers.

All this on a windy beach, with the constant chatter of the defendant in the background.

It is work like this that is an inspiration to prosecutors everywhere.

Sex in the Dock

Dear John

For prosecutors having criticism levelled against us is just part of the job but to be accused of being out of touch is unfair. We are just as much on the ball now as we have always been. Aren't we?

I would say there has been a marked improvement going by the reported cases.

In 1960 at the Old Bailey, Penguin faced

prosecution under the Obscene Publications Act for its publication of *Lady Chatterley's Lover* by D.H. Lawrence who had died in 1930.

In the book, Lady Chatterley has an affair with her husband's gamekeeper as her husband is unable to have sexual intercourse due to a WW1 injury.

Did the book tend to deprave and corrupt? If so, was its publication 'for the public good' on the grounds of its literary merits?

Apart from the "f" word being used 30 times, the Prosecutor listed sexual intercourse taking place "thirteen times" including in "her husband's house,...a hut,...the undergrowth,...when stark naked and dripping with raindrops..." He concluded, "And finally...we have it all over again in the attic in a Bloomsbury boarding-house."

The prosecutor asked, "Would you approve of your... young daughters – because girls can read as well as boys – reading this book?... Is it a book that you would even wish your wife or servants to read?"

The defence said that society cannot fix its standards by what is suitable for a 14-year-old.

Over a six-day trial there were a number of witnesses, including:

1. Author Rebecca West who gave evidence that the book had literary merit, but was badly written by a man who had no sense of humour and no background of education in his home.

2. The Bishop of Woolwich who agreed that Christians ought to read it. This led to the headline in the evening papers, "A Book all Christians should read".

I'll Have the Law on You

The defence contended that Shakespeare's Antony and Cleopatra may as well have been a "story of a sex-starved man copulating with an Egyptian Queen."

The judge summed up suggesting that the jury think of "factory girls reading in their lunchtime."

After a six-day trial, the jury found Penguin not guilty.

OMwards and Upwards

Dear John,

As a reward for long government service, I have been offered the job of Ombudsman. However, it sounds a little bit too challenging so near to my retirement. I am concerned that it may be too taxing and argumentative.

In the days of old, there were knights who were bold. Nevertheless, there were also many knights who just pottered around their castles and occasionally girded their loins to attend banquets. Whether they lacked

inclination or funds, they were still knights. Such is the power of branding.

The Ombudsman is not an advocate for complainants nor is he there to stick up for government departments. He is somewhere in the politically correct but potentially ineffective middle. Doing anything while maintaining your independence with both sides can be difficult. Therefore, doing nothing can be an attractive and sensible option for some Ombudsmen, bearing in mind that most complainants could be classified as last resort crackpots.

Here are seven habits that will make you a highly ineffective but relatively snug Ombudsman:

1. *Try to close complaints without doing anything at all. This is easier than you think.*

2. *Increase complaint numbers by accepting complaints by telephone, email, website, even twitter, anonymous or otherwise. Vague complaints are easier to close.*

3. *Do not identify and properly resource complaints that have merit. Treat them all the same and spread your resources thinly so that you can be seen to be dealing with each one fairly, albeit ineffectively.*

4. *Leverage complaints. If the complaint is made too early it can be opened, and then closed, and then reopened again once the time has arrived for the complaint to be received. Thus, one complaint becomes statistically two complaints.*

5. *Do not have customer satisfaction surveys unless you are forced to do so. Put testimonials on your website and issue loads of statistics.*

I'll Have the Law on You

6. *Offer training to government departments on how they can deal cheerfully but not too effectively with complaints. This will create further statistics and keep your staff fully occupied.*

7. *Some ungrateful complainants may complain about you too. Label these as vexatious so that no one takes any notice of them.*

As a safe, reticent bureaucratic pair of hands, you will be considered perfect for the position.

Join Your Local Witch Hunt

Dear John,

I could have been a contender. Is there still time for me to push my weight around a bit, leave a legacy?

Those of us who have not followed life with sufficient gravitas to become a judge can always righteously adopt a serious cause and seek elevation to a commission or investigating committee. For others with a shorter attention span, the advent of social media offers mobs opportunities that

Thomas Paine and French revolutionaries could only dream of.

In 1953 *The Crucible*, a play by Arthur Miller, likened the House Un-American Activities Committee (HUAC) to the Salem Witch Trials of 1692. Hollywood operated a blacklist for celebrities falling foul of the HUAC such as Charlie Chaplin, Orson Welles and Paul Robeson, all of whom had to go overseas to work.

Miller was suspected of being a communist and in 1954 the HUAC denied him a passport for the London opening of his play.

In 1956 Miller married Marilyn Monroe and was subpoenaed to appear before the HUAC. Miller did not wish to name names and the Chairman seemed to agree to defer that question. Miller then gave an account of his own involvement with Communism as a writer under a pseudonym. He was later convicted of contempt for refusing to name names and was sentenced to a fine of $500 or 30 days imprisonment. He was blacklisted and disallowed a US passport. He appealed and his conviction was overturned as the Chairman's concession made it unclear that a prosecution would follow.

Witch hunts are just as popular today, be it retired light entertainment celebrities, priests, climate change sceptics or anybody appearing to step over the bounds of political correctness. Everyone is entitled to an opinion on these topics provided it is the right one or they keep it to themselves, otherwise they are attacked too. Names (right or wrong) are named and vilified.

Amid this are people like Miller who dared to lampoon, and Napoleon who perhaps more satisfyingly turned the cannon on the mob, while sensible people do nothing and keep their opinions to themselves.

What can you do about it? Well, if you are like me, nothing.

I'll Have the Law on You

Being Put Out to Grass

Dear John,

After 25 years and several mergers, I have found myself a partner at a large law firm which has decided to put me out to grass, a little bit like *Logan's Run*. They have done so in a kindly, strategic manner and have given me an extremely generous severance package. I feel obliged to take it and go quietly rather than going legal.

Except for sexual harassment, which at your age is understandably not an issue, going legal is too predictable.

There is a true story about an old miser in a small village in Germany who was very unpopular. When he died, he left a will that gave generously to every single person in the village. The will provided funds for a wake to which all the villagers were invited. The deceased was to be dressed in his best suit and laid out on his bed so that the villagers could pay their respects.

The villagers went to his cottage, trooped up the stairs and stood around

his bed. Just as someone had started to say that he wasn't so bad after all, there was a loud crash, the floorboards gave way and several villagers were killed.

The old miser had sawn away the joists underneath the floorboards.

Not only does this illustrate just one of the many advantages of having a will, it shows that revenge can be a coping mechanism when contemplating your own death.

After 25 years, you will have a corner (hopefully upstairs) office, coveted by every other lawyer in the firm. Immediately, after your departure they will all rush to your office to lay their respective claims...

Going gentle into that goodnight may be your most sensible option, but it is not your only option.

PART 5

COUPLES COMPLAINING ABOUT THEIR ADULT CHILDREN AND EACH OTHER

Fytit answered the need in most families to complain about each other by providing timely and empathetic legal advice.

Leaving Your Spouse Out of Your Will

Dear John,

My spouse is devoted to me but I worry that in grief at my death, my spouse will fall easy prey to some fortune hunter. Of course, I would not begrudge some happiness

42

after my passing but what if my spouse dies and leaves everything to this chancer's children?

Whether you have worked hard to earn it, had the good fortune to have someone leave it to you or just spent the last 40 years bored witless watching your spouse amass it, your concern is understandable.

We all from time to time consider leaving our money directly to our children expecting our spouses to understand. They generally don't. In fact, they expect the children to see sense and renounce their windfall. Naturally, your children respect your wishes.

If you adopt this strategy there are risks:

- You can expect your spouse to sue the estate. Such cases often settle but only after acrimonious affidavits full of accusations about your sanity, bad temper and slovenly habits. Fortunately, this is all done in confidence, it is not as if your neighbours and friends get to read the unpleasant detail. Unless, of course, they are called as witnesses.

- I would suggest that you make your own funeral arrangements just in case your spouse decides to cut a few corners.

- Above all, you must not allow your spouse to know of your intentions in case they decide to do the same thing. Whereas they need to be saved from themselves, you probably feel that you can be trusted to leave the money to your kids. Unless your children marry unwisely or forget to call you on your birthday.

To look on the bright side, you are long gone before the fighting starts. Neverthless, if you cannot stand to have your memory besmirched in this manner but still fear your money ending up with the wrong person, there really is only one option. Don't go.

Married and Bored *

Dear John,

I am married to a lawyer and he is very boring. Is it true that old lawyers never die they just lose their appeal?

Being married to a lawyer myself for over 30 years, I can confirm that they are exceedingly dull but, like an old Labrador, very affable.

Consider yourself lucky that he can't count. Otherwise, you may have ended up married to an accountant or banker.

Thought to be from Fytit's wife.

The Family Lawyer

Dear John,

Our family has had the same lawyer for years. However, in his efforts to be even-handed, he seems to be giving equal weight to the views of my daughter-in-law even when they contradict my own.

The days of the genial lawyer steering generations of the same family through their legal affairs are gone. We have had to specialise as family members have become more self-centred and unwilling to follow the guidance of their matriarch.

There are specialist lawyers for each member of the family. One national law firm, Drinking Works has gone after the trillion dollar "wastrel sons" market. The moment it got out that interviews were held in the local bar starting at lunchtime, the work dried up for the rest of us.

I have had to re-organise my firm and have decided to target the "unappreciated husbands and fathers" market that has long needed an

advocate. I am considering rebranding my firm to Wife Works that I believe will have appeal to many husbands. I dismissed the idea of Child at Uni Works after several trials.

With both husband and wife separately represented, Saturday night arguments would need to be rescheduled to office hours, leading to increasingly peaceful "off the record" weekends. A wife's alleged nagging would take the form of carefully crafted letters and result in less repetition and bad language. A detailed and accurate record of the husband's failings would be available for later court proceedings and the wife's friends over coffee.

What slightly crazed and cranky uncle would not be happier with an equally irrational lawyer being irritated on his behalf? Larger law firms could stop hiding such practitioners or forcing them into practice on their own.

With animal rights' specialists, finally the family dog could demand rather than beg.

A mother-in-law specialist could give you the support and empathy that you need.

Shouting

Dear John,

I have just married a lawyer and found that the shouting actually increased after the wedding. Do all lawyers shout and is there anything that I can do about it?

Part 5

Not all lawyers shout. There are lawyers who prefer malevolent silences, only sometimes accompanied by angry outbursts called judges.

But the law does seem to be full of people who do not listen. It can be due to arrogance, but more often it is the result of extreme deafness or, for people listening to a lawyer, tuning out. Therefore, when making an important point, shouting can be a useful tool.

You may find that with the passing of the years your spouse changes. Often with lawyers, it is not for the better.

Therefore, it is an inside job, acceptance being the key. As you get older, you may find the shouting motivational and informative, rather than irritating.

On reflection, it may be best to get out now.

GREAT LAW SCHOOLS OF THE DEEP

47

I'll Have the Law on You

Influencing Adult Children

Dear John,

Is there any legal way I can make my children face up to their responsibilities and show me some attention?

Any mention of your will should do the trick.

Find a worthy cause to champion. Your lawyer will have a whole book of charitable institutions. My advice is to opt for the slightly offbeat. My own clients have become very fond of a local donkey sanctuary.

A word of caution: do not leave your money to your own pet. It is a certain death sentence. Unless, of course, your pet shows you no attention either.

Use a codicil, a short addition to a will, in order to write out any particular offender. Alternatively, announce that you intend to make a new will to shake up all of your children.

With a bit of thought, your next Mother's Day could be a very special occasion indeed.

THE READING OF THE WILL

Part 5

Challenging a Will *

Dear John,

I have decided not to leave most of my $56B to my three children. Could they challenge the will?

Your children would be advised to consider three different arguments:

1. *Their dad is nuts. This is increasingly popular.*

2. *They are still dependant on their dad. This seems to work at any age; parents never seem to make adequate provision.*

3. *Their dad's lawyers messed up the terms of the will. This is an argument that we understandably try to discourage.*

Allegations of frequent loss of car keys, forgetting names and having no idea of where a car is parked are dismissed by most judges as normal behaviour. However, I suspect trying to convince any judge that

someone who gives away $56B is entirely rational would be an uphill struggle, especially if you tried to maintain that it was your wife's idea.

What is adequate provision? Well, $56B would do it, but anything less may be the subject of a challenge.

I suspect your children would prefer the whole inheritance neatly divided three ways as most of us do.

Rather than leave my own children locked in expensive and divisive litigation, I have decided to take the advice I normally give to my own clients and spend it before I go. I shall leave a note explaining that it was for their own good.

* Thought to be Bill Gates of Microsoft.

Part 5

Naughty Sons – Advice to Mothers

Dear John,

I have always been very proud of my son but now he tells me that he wants to put me in a home. How do I explain to him that I don't wish to go?

You are not alone. Many parents live under the yoke of their adult children. They tend not to show it but engage in a campaign of civil disobedience in collaboration with their grandchildren e.g. buying peeing puppies, financing vomit inducing chocolate binges and permitting late and inappropriate movie sessions etc. Grandparents can find combining this with breaking wind at inopportune moments very satisfying.

Sons, often egged on by wicked daughters-in-law, start to give hints about retirement homes at any time after their parent's 55th birthday.

Your lawyer will advise you of the 5 point "We Are Staying Put, Son" ("WASPS") strategy. Use this to make your son's interjections into your

TROLLEY RAGE...
IT WAS HIS LUCKY DAY

51

life a less pleasurable experience for him until he backs off.

1. Hide all family heirlooms, rings, carpets, watches etc., to stop him visiting you just for the pleasure of inspecting them and declaring which ones will be his.

2. If you cannot bring yourself to find an outspoken lesbian lover, invent one.

3. Adopt a "poison will" clause. This is similar to the "poison pill" strategy that companies use to avoid takeovers. You incorporate a clause in your will that leaves your son's share of your estate to someone else. Even rich sons will baulk at the thought of their inheritance being left to say, a donkey sanctuary.

4. Stop taking handouts from your son. Bolster your income by taking in washing, playing more bingo, seeking out senior bargains or by simply taking a rich and preferably childless lover.

5. Avoid displays of aggressive hatred, especially those that lead to police involvement. Any sign of mental instability may enable your son to take over your affairs. Psychiatrists will be on your son's side; they have parents themselves.

If your son prevails, a retirement home beats being put out on the ice. So do not give him any ideas.

THE MAN IN THE ARENA

It is not the critic who counts; not the man who points out how the strong man stumbles, or where the doer of deeds could have done them better. The credit belongs to the man who is actually in the arena, whose face is marred by dust and sweat and blood; who strives valiantly; who errs, who comes short again and again, because there is no effort without error and shortcoming; but who does actually strive to do the deeds; who knows great enthusiasms, the great devotions; who spends himself in a worthy cause; who at the best knows in the end the triumph of high achievement, and who at the worst, if he fails, at least fails while daring greatly, so that his place shall never be with those cold and timid souls who neither know victory nor defeat.

Theodore Roosevelt
26th President of the United States

PART 6

ADULT CHILDREN CONCERNED ABOUT THEIR INHERITANCE BEING MISMANAGED

This was a very common theme.

Will Anybody Rid Me of This Turbulent Mother-in-Law?

Dear John,

My mother-in-law (MIL) is an interfering old harridan, you know the type.

She has just written a book entitled *My Son Married a Prize Bitch*. Her publisher says that it will be a best seller. Can I sue?

Part 6

Many MILs have a tense relationship with their daughters-in-law (DILs) despite having once been DILs themselves. However, with the arrival of grandchildren, MILs usually manage to contain their animosity to gain generous access, and in return provide financial support together with baby-sitting services. To sue, would risk losing these benefits.

It is better to maintain a close relationship with your in-laws while at the same time implementing a Wealth Early Transfer (WET) strategy:

a. Debt Assistance

In-laws may be prepared to guarantee your outstanding debts, especially from a failed business venture. This will enable you to increase your spending but is usually accompanied by unwanted advice.

b. Joint Business Venture

It is easier to involve your in-laws in the business venture itself from the beginning. Think big and you may be able to persuade them to sell their home and move in with you, ideally in accommodation accompanying the venture. If the business flourishes, you will find yourself able to put up with your MIL, but if it falters, you can throw a tantrum and lock them out. Place the business on the market and if you have chosen wisely, the sale could take years.

Considering school fees, foreign travel and all the other expenses of having children these days, it is inadvisable to fall out with, let alone sue your in-laws.

Look on the bright side, the royalties of her new book could be yours one day.

I'll Have the Law on You

Your Inheritance – Is it in Safe Hands?

Dear John,

From a legal point of view, does it matter which of your parents dies first?

I am asked this more and more by adult children now that euthanasia is lawful in certain parts of the world.

I think we should take a tip from nature where the male generally goes first. This is because the death of a spouse can feel like a release for many fathers. It allows them to pursue a drunken and extravagantly reckless old age, funded by your inheritance and often involving some floozy.

A mother on the other hand tends to lead a quiet life, contemplating the happy years spent with her departed husband. Unless of course, he has not left her enough money. Then there is a good chance that she will go all out to find a rich substitute. A mother can irrationally believe that if she does not perform, you, her adult son, may put her in

Part 6

a home or some budget accommodation. Perhaps I am exaggerating here, as you may not listen to your spouse at all about the budget accommodation, but you get the point.

If your mother chooses wisely and manages to outlive the second husband, there is a good chance that she will inherit his money and leave it all to you. It may be better at that stage to cash in while you are ahead and have your mother put your inheritance in a trust for your benefit, to ward off any gold digging third husbands.

Therefore, legally, it is best for your dad to head off first. Keep your mother going with regular exercise. Lock up the chocolates and restrict gin to the usual Friday night session.

Parents Not Coping With Finances

Dear John,

My parents are getting on and I am concerned that they are no longer able to exercise their usual prudent financial rigour for the assets they have amassed. This is of particular concern to me, as I have inherited only "right brain" artistic type genes. Money has not really interested me up until now, but I would be extremely distressed if it stopped short.

I'll Have the Law on You

Should I take on some of the burden of managing my parents' finances?

Most children believe that their parents are well meaning but a little daft. Or is that just my children? Parents are not to be trusted with decisions concerning your inheritance as the consequences of a wrong move can have serious implications for you. They could go completely gaga and spend it! Therefore, you must get involved. Once you start applying estate planning principles to your parents' money rather than your own, it becomes a fascinating subject.

Smart Phones and the Law

Dear John,

A court has ruled that a will can be made on a smart phone. My parents can be a little impulsive. How do I stop my inheritance being lost on a whim?

It used to be that thieves were branded on the cheek, murderers were hanged, and if a will was not signed at the bottom or foot thereof in the presence of two witnesses present at the same time, it was not valid. We all knew where

LAWYERS CALL IN CONSULTANTS TO DEVISE ALTERNATIVE TO BILLALBLE HOUR

we stood. Although it was difficult to get a will executed without someone inadvertently trying to leave the room or wanting to sign in the wrong place, we managed. Now, if a Testator had a clear intention of creating a will despite not observing the legal niceties, a judge may allow it over the line.

Once a Testator is deceased, it is no longer his wife who decides his intentions for him. A judge decides his intentions, so it can go either way. This means that if those in charge of your inheritance are unreliable (and let's face it, we are dealing with your parents here) you may need to have an entire court case to beat off the other claimants. That can be expensive.

Therefore, it is best that you pay for your parents to make their wills properly and then wipe them out before they change their minds. This is not without risk, and care should be taken to avoid suspicion of patricide, matricide or the ever popular, step-matricide. However, no one is surprised by what parents get up to these days. Accidents involving Bucking Broncos, parachuting and micro lighting seem commonplace for the over 70s.

To protect your inheritance you need to be vigilant and proactive. It may not be enough to support your parents' extreme lifestyle choices and wait.

I'll Have the Law on You

The Importance of Receiving Correctly

Dear John,

My elderly, rich uncle is dying but has such a dislike of lawyers, he refuses to make a will. As his closest and dearest relative, I am naturally concerned about this crazy notion.

My experience is that once people reach 55 they seem to spend a lot of time dying or at least mentioning signs of decline. Rich people can be the worst offenders, often outliving caring neighbours only to make a will decades later in favour of the 50 something blond across the road. It is important to make sure that your uncle is definitely on his way out, and not just a tyre kicker.

His verbal assurance is of no use, you need it in writing. It is often difficult to find the right time to bring this up. Yet, is it too much trouble for him to give it to you as gift before he goes? Of course, this would probably cause tax issues for you but it may help him to know that you are ready to make sacrifices too.

Intestacy – Thinking Outside the Box

Dear John,

My elderly cousin is dying and it looks as if I am the closest relative. He will not make a will as he hates lawyers (he used to be married to one) but he says that he wants me to inherit. His property is in various states and countries.

Clearly, your cousin is traumatised by his choice of spouse. This is not uncommon.

If he dies without a will, his estate will be subject to the laws of intestacy which can be a lottery. Without a will, some countries or states may not recognize the place of a cousin in the pecking order. This could mean that you would not inherit property located in that state or country.

Therefore, it is important to research where his assets are located and encourage your cousin to sell any inconveniently located assets. Your lawyer can help you with this paperwork.

HE HAD TRIED TO TELL THE RELATIVES THAT IT WAS TOO LATE

I'll Have the Law on You

It may be necessary to relocate your cousin to a more convenient jurisdiction that fully recognises your claim. If he is awkward, (dying, rich relatives can be particularly miserable and selfish) it is best to leave the transfer to the last minute in order to minimise any unpleasant scenes.

What happens if he dies in transit? Well, it depends if anybody notices.

PART 7

ADVICE ON ISSUES RAISED BY PEOPLE WITH NOTHING BETTER TO DO

Defriend or Foe?

Dear John,

On Facebook there is a person who I wish to defriend. Could defriending be defamatory? Does it amount to an imputation that there is something wrong with that person? Would it be safer to write to the person first, setting out my reasons so that they can make submissions before I take the decision to defriend?

LAWYERS EMBRACE SOCIAL MEDIA

Absolutely not, but have you considered the more satisfying and rewarding alternative of commencing legal proceedings?

A writ could be posted on your Friend's timeline. Rather than being vindictive, you could claim you were just being efficient as it is now sometimes possible to serve court documents via Facebook. Others may Like the Post and if your Friend is particularly unpopular, it could go viral on Twitter. The writ could be boosted by a tasteful, paid Facebook advertisement. Something as mundane as a neighbourhood tree dispute could attract thousands of visitors to your Facebook page.

If this proves popular, you may find yourself eyeing up other Friends to sue. Of course, it would be best to choose your targets with the benefit of advice from a lawyer who practices in the area of anti-social media, as I do. It is a matter of trial and error, but accountants and bankers have proved extremely popular targets for my clients.

Therefore, it is essential to remain Facebook Friends so that your Friend can not only witness the humiliation of being so publically vilified, but also be subject to the added sting of suspecting that they have helped to improve your social media standing.

As the Godfather said, "Keep your friends close but your Facebook Friends closer."

Part 7

Dull and Duller

Dear John,

Is social media for me?

I always supported Facebook's quest to create increasingly accurate algorithms so that users would only be subjected to highly targeted advertising. Until that is, the advertisement for "singles" on the side of my Facebook page was replaced by an advertisement for a pair of sensible brown shoes.

Rather than a targeted promotion, I suspect that this was the work of some fresh faced youngster at Facebook, pressed to re-categorize the entire legal profession before the pizza was delivered.

However, could the young lady who depressingly offered me her seat on the train be part of this conspiracy? Why when a client asked, "I bet your Jag goes some", did I reply, "I wouldn't know"? How is it that just before Christmas last year, I left work at 5pm, went to two cocktail parties, and still arrived home by 7.20pm?

THE "HANGING JUDGE JEFFREYS IS COOL" GROUP HAD BECOME VERY POPULAR

65

I'll Have the Law on You

This fine-tuning of algorithms may also explain the ubiquitous appearance of Volvo adverts in my world.

If it continues in this way, Facebook will soon find, as so many lawyers have done prosecuting or defending, that the truth is sometimes an inconvenient and unwelcome hurdle to client satisfaction.

Death of Social Media

Dear John,

Should I be concerned about my Facebook account after I die?

To manage your social media commitments when you have a business to run is difficult. When you are dead, it becomes almost impossible. However, with the right social media strategy, your Virtual Assistant in Mumbai will live on and continue to send out your posts at one o'clock in the morning and even change your status to "PO" ("passed on").

Nowadays, people have Facebook Friends that they do not know from

Adam. This creates special challenges for executors who feel that they must ensure Friends are aware of your death but also want access to your profile to discover who you were. Therefore, the executors need quick access to secure control and utilize your online information. Leaving a Digital Register of all your assets and passwords to access the assets would be useful, or even just a list of the passwords to your social media accounts. Yet, as you cannot remember the passwords yourself, it is probably not going to happen.

If executors are ready to do battle with privacy issues, they can increase your Likes but do not expect them to attract many followers.

To paraphrase Johnny Carson - for three days after death, hair and fingernails continue to grow but tweets taper off.

I'll Have the Law on You

Empty Jails

Dear John,

With the creeping de-criminalisation of drugs and falling crime rates, will our prisons soon be empty?

There has never been a shortage of people to persecute and incarcerate. I am sure we will think of something. For instance, many in the legal profession have always felt that children, especially teenagers, would gain from a custodial sentence. I am not suggesting long sentences (except in certain cases). Sentences would mostly take place in the school holidays so as not to interfere with schoolwork. There would be no criminal records as the Child Custody ("CC") System would not deal with crimes but everyday family irritations, such as talking back and eating with elbows on the table. Not every infraction would result in imprisonment. For instance, what teenage son would refuse to put out the garbage if he had a suspended sentence hanging over his head? Only the consent of the parents would be required. I expect that in most cases, this would

SPORTSWEAR FOR ACCOUNTANTS

be enthusiastically given, especially for Holiday CC.

Once the principle was established, it could extend to other troublesome family members such as mothers-in-law. Forcibly sending your mother-in-law to prison may be a breach of her human rights. However, human rights' lawyers have never defended mothers-in-law in the past, and I suspect that they would not start now.

Once the criminals were cleared out of the prison system, wives could be attracted by a high-security diet that really worked. Fathers may seek some solitude, especially leading up to Christmas and weddings. No household chores, requests for money or shopping expeditions for even short periods could be a welcome respite.

Include a "Throw Away the Key" option for spouses and we will need more prisons not less.

I'll Have the Law on You

Falling Crime Rates

Dear John,

Are falling crimes rates just another sign of the unreliability of this generation?

A growing number of prosecutors blame computer games such as Grand Theft Auto and Call of Duty that have enticed the young to play out their violent, rapacious fantasies in the comfort of their own bedrooms rather than on the streets. One Attorney General told me, "We were against violent computer games when they were first introduced and we are against them now; we are just less sure of why."

Psychologists attribute the cause to the increase in single parent families that often lack the presence of a violent father as a role model. Also, working mothers are just too tired and no longer at home to terrorise their teenage children and drive them out onto the streets.

While authoritarian governments see the absence of youth on the streets as a good thing, other governments have

THE MAGISTRATE COULD BE VERY RUDE TO YOUNG ADVOCATES

coped with the decline by pretending that crime rates are going up, in keeping with the public's perception.

Parents who in the past have relied on their teenage children to bring home the bacon and anything else that they could lay their hands on, are facing financial hardship. The issue is compounded by their own parents who are retiring earlier and earlier, demanding attention and financial support. The solution is for retired parents to undertake shoplifting and mugging duties. Governments could set a generous limit to the amount that retired parents can steal before their Age Pensions are reduced.

Falling crime rates could be reversed by the adjustment of existing laws. For instance, change "threatening behaviour" to "looking at me in a funny way" and leave the rest up to police discretion. Who would not applaud the application of the terrorism laws to telemarketers?

By combining these simple changes with an increase in police numbers and a return to trumped up charges, the courts will be as busy as ever and no longer reliant on degenerate youth.

I'll Have the Law on You

Marriage and Death

Dear John,

There has been a decline in marriage's popularity that started, for many of us, immediately after the wedding. Many heterosexual couples now avoid it altogether. Will gay marriage revitalise the institution?

With the current divorce rate hovering at around 50%, gay marriage will give a much-needed boost to the married community's numbers. However, an unintended consequence could be an increase in the Matrimonial Murder Rate ("MMR").

Disturbingly, 38% of murdered women are killed by their husbands. Often, wives are strangled in the bedroom whereas husbands are stabbed in the kitchen. Hence, the increasing popularity of knife blocks.

Of course, the introduction of same-sex married couples could even things up and reduce the MMR by making it less likely that one party could overwhelm the other, a

Part 7

sort of Matrimonial Mutually Assured Destruction ("MMAD").

Further improvement to the MMR could be achieved by the introduction of polygamy to give married women backup. Saturday night fights between couples could become all night tag fixtures enjoyed by the whole family and neighbours alike. Same-sex polygamy would allow fanatical football supporters to demonstrate their commitment by marrying and settling down with the entire team, giving the rest of us a break.

I asked my wife, "How many husbands do you think are murdered by their wives?" and she replied, "Not enough." I may need back up.

The Grim Eater

Dear John,

I was very distressed to hear that in New Zealand, funeral directors had noticed that a quiet, respectable looking man in his 40's wearing a suit, was attending up to four funerals a week. Some had reported that he took away food in plastic containers. Newspapers reported that the "Grim Eater" was eventually taken aside by a funeral director and given a stiff talking to.

I'll Have the Law on You

Surely this can only serve to drive up the cost of funerals for us senior citizens?

Dishonestly taking funeral refreshments belonging to another without consent is theft.

This is not an uncommon problem, especially where the deceased was unpopular and the relatives, desperate to get bums on pews, did not carefully vet attendees.

In these circumstances, I suggest that you avoid general invitations to mourners such as, "You are all welcome to join us for refreshments afterwards." This is implied consent and a defence to a charge of theft. It is probably better to say nothing as choosing the right words can be difficult. Words such as "Will friends of the deceased..." could exclude many attendees, especially ex-spouses.

A refreshment ticketing system often used at accountants' funerals is ideal, and particularly useful in the event of a tax office audit.

Another argument used by sandwich stealers, especially great aunts, is that the sandwiches are left over and therefore it is permissible to take them away. A small tasteful sign saying "Food must be consumed on the premises" is useful evidence. Nevertheless, if the sandwiches are to be thrown away, legally it could mean that they belong to no one, which is a defence to theft. In the case of left over sandwiches, it is difficult to get the Funeral Director to give evidence that they would have been re-circulated at the next funeral. Therefore, a "doggy bag" clause in the funeral contract would be further evidence that the sandwiches were not abandoned.

A trespasser once discovered, can be asked to leave and ejected with reasonable force. If forcible ejection is necessary, it is best to

Part 7

have the trespasser dragged rather than lifted up onto shoulders. This avoids any claims of injury against the estate by over-enthusiastic mourners or the trespasser themselves.

Gossiping-the Do's and Don'ts

Dear John,

I admit that I am a good communicator, but to label me a gossip is both hurtful and defamatory. I am a caring person and if I do pass on information, it is for the good of the community even when it turns out to be wrong. Alternatively, it is entertaining tittle-tattle. Surely the law is not taking away the basic right of a chat between acquaintances, however distant?

The victims of gossip, understandably often turn out to have no sense of humour about it at all.

If you have gone too far, a quick apology, given and accepted, is the best course of action for all parties. The alternative is to wait and see if the victim will sue you for defamation, which can be a successful strategy depending on the seriousness of your defamatory

statements. Lawyers and probably spouses can help even stubborn people to assess the stupidity of their statements.

You could claim "qualified privilege" in that you acted reasonably, not recklessly in making the defamatory statement, even if it turned out to be wrong. A court will consider if it was your duty to make the statement e.g. a member of your staff had a terrible secret, or it was in the public interest e.g. your mother-in-law is an axe murderer. The person you tell must also have a need to know. For instance, your mother-in-law's next-door neighbour probably does not need to know about your employee's secret, but may find it useful to know about your mother-in-law being an axe murderer.

You must act sensibly and check your source. If it is someone who is unreliable or as big a gossip as you, then it may be best not to pass it on, especially if it will have serious consequences e.g. your mother-in-law's arrest, detention and trial, even if she is eventually acquitted.

PART 8

GENERAL IRRITATIONS OF LIFE

Other Peoples' Children

Dear John,

Parents are so boastful of their childrens' achievements. Does such irritating behaviour offend against any law? I do not say this just because my own childrens' achievements have been modest.

Being an irritating parent is not an offence. My wife and I attended a parents' evening where one mother was concerned that the curriculum would not challenge her child as he was academically gifted. Later, the mother questioned the adequacy of the sports facilities as the boy was a natural

I'll Have the Law on You

athlete. Finally, her hand was up again to question the music teacher as her son was also a talented musician. He was 7 years old. As my wife later commented, "It is amazing that the most gifted children have the most stupid mothers."

Not Enough Money

Dear John,

I have not made a will as I am too embarrassed to reveal how little I have. I always hoped that something would turn up, but time is running out.

Most people are reluctant to admit how little they have accumulated. Therefore, it is quite acceptable to lie about it. It took me a few depressing years before I realised that my clients did not have more money than I did; they just said that they did.

Over the years they have:

- Invented rich uncles poised to leave them a fortune.

Part 8

- Made out that they have so much money they do not need to work.

- Claimed that they have given substantial sums to charity.

Some clients got carried away, hinting at expensive mistresses and rich, generous mothers-in-law.

All fantasy of course.

Billing and Wills

Dear John,

My lawyer has nagged me for years about making a will. He said it was one of the cheapest legal things I could do. I finally gave him instructions but he expressed no joy at my change of heart. He then charged me like there was no tomorrow. What's going on?

In the past, there was always an unspoken understanding that a client, having made a will, would do the right thing and promptly fall off the perch. Now, even clients who have every intention of pegging it seem to hang on.

79

I'll Have the Law on You

Medical practice has changed. It used to be three score years and ten and that was your lot. Now doctors seem to go all out to keep people going. Losing a few patients here and there is no longer acceptable to the medical profession. Doctors say that they are just trying to meet the expectations of relatives, elevated after watching hospital dramas.

Worse still, clients are being encouraged by well-meaning financial planners and others in the finance industry, to make wills long before they have any intention of dying at all.

Therefore, will prices, traditionally based on a quick turnaround, have had to go up. Some firms keep prices down by offering an Early Bird Discount to try to attract the more serious players who, although dying, still find it hard to resist a bargain.

Try telling your lawyer that you have not been feeling well. It may help.

Part 8

Cats and the Law

Dear John,

Despite having a cat door, my cat wakes me up every night wanting to be let in and out. My sleep is being severely disturbed. Is it illegal to kill a cat?

Cats do not have nine lives. This old adage is a reference to failed assassination attempts by their owners, so you are not alone. My own cat has a permanent scowl.

Your cat is your property and you can kill it, provided it is not done in a cruel manner. For instance, drowning it in a bucket, although quick, is prohibited as an extreme form of water boarding. Even a pillow placed gently over its face, after it has dozed for 20 hours straight in its favourite chair, may be considered cruel in the cold light of the courtroom.

Therefore, it is best left to your vet. Yet, most vets (not all) are animal lovers. They treat requests for execution of a healthy, albeit

malevolent animal as motivated by cruel intent. This is why many regimes when dealing with subversives, use "trumped up" charges. As the vet's determination is behind closed doors with no witnesses, no investigation and no appeal, accusations of attacks on pregnant mothers, babies, widows or as a last resort, puppies should work fairly well. As many cats have a nightlife that Hannibal Lecter would be proud of, the vet should be easily convinced that they are dealing with an enemy of the state. Any delay on their part may result in a lawsuit against them by one of the victims.

Nonetheless, your cat's untimely death may not improve your sleep. Guilt may weigh upon you as it did with Lady Macbeth. Alternatively, your small triumph may result in you turning on other members of your family who are even more irritating.

If you have reached an age where you find that your only nemesis is your cat, it probably means that you should get out more. At least, that is my plan.

Part 8

Car Parking Space Abuse

Dear John

Will car parking space law ever develop to provide the protection that is so overdue?

There is that time in a movie when the mild mannered citizen finally cracks and seeks retribution. This is how I felt the other morning when someone parked in my car parking space. In Queensland, we do not strap on our Colt 45, or load up our shotgun we use stickers.

Despite being red, bearing the word **WARNING**, containing threats of a financial penalty and the car being towed away stickers have proven less effective than lynching.

One problem is that the sticker repeats the same threats that appear on the Warning Sign which the offender ignored on the way into the car park. To be effective threats must escalate. For instance, attach a rock to a sticker bearing the words "We know where you live".

If your Warning Sign is being ignored ditch the

legalese and put something more compelling such as "Ebola Research Centre".

Victims are urged not to place the sticker on the windscreen but on a side window so that the offender's line of sight is not impaired during the getaway. Whereas victims call for poster sized Warning Stickers.

At midday I looked out the window, the offending car was gone and I reclaimed my space. It was then that three things occurred to me:

1. It had been the morning of our trust account audit;

2. The auditor had left just before noon; and

3. As I had stuck the sticker on the windscreen I was impressed by the neatness of the car interior.

Whether or not it was a friendly fire sticker incident, we will hopefully never know.

Would it help to give Warning Stickers legal authority? Yes, but only if there was someone (possibly a masked stranger) ready to enforce such laws against wrong doers.

Neighbours

Dear John,

I know God says love thy neighbour and I have tried, but I can't stand mine. I don't like his dog, his loud wife, his noisy kids and most of all his big mouth. We have almost come to blows on several occasions. Please help.

Of course, we all feel like this about our neighbours but we manage to confine our hostility to the occasional sneaky attack.

Start building a legal case. You need independent witnesses (no relatives). If you have a video camera, use it.

A video of your neighbour shouting is good, especially if there are threats of violence. However, what you are really looking for is some violence towards you or, more preferably, your wife.

Will your neighbour's criminal trial and conviction be the end of the matter? Of course not, but some would view it as a very satisfying start.

I'll Have the Law on You

Glossy But Dull

Dear John,

The glossy information sheet that accompanied my new driving licence warned me to "try and keep it flat", "not to deform it by cutting or hitting it" and "not to soak it". Increasingly, my attention is diverted by pointless information packaged in a way that invites attention. The duller the message, the greater the marketing subterfuge. Can the law offer any solution to these time wasting antics?

All content should be colour coded red, white or blue. Red being worth reading, white being devote your usual attention and blue being not worth reading. For instance, all legal documents produced by banks would be defaulted to blue with occasional white and red streaks to enable customers to hone in on the important parts and disregard the rest. Productivity would increase dramatically.

Then we could colour code our politicians and have three parliaments, blue being not worth listening to. Materials,

Part 8

red, white, or blue produced by politicians of any hue, would be removed to the appropriate parliament.

With colour coded TV channels, all the films and shows which received bad reviews would be shown on a blue channel, giving us all the opportunity to have evenings free of the usual rubbish.

There would be anomalies. For instance, some blue jokes would need to be reclassified as red, and red herrings would become blue. Brides would aspire to red weddings.

In order to enforce these laws, white and blue judges would be appointed to join the red judges. Cases would be allocated red, white or blue status purely on entertainment value.

Younger Sisters as Bridesmaids

Dear John,

I am worried that my younger sister will try to upstage me on my wedding day. Legally, how can I stop her? *

Younger sisters can be selfish. However, rather than causing family upset by barring her from the wedding, a Deed of Indenture would allow

87

you to stipulate certain things. For instance, how many times she could bend down to pick up your train and a minimum bridesmaid weight requirement to prevent excessive dieting. A provision for a weigh-in the night before the wedding can be quite fun.

The Deed could also provide appropriate standards for the bridesmaid's dress. A carefully worded Undergarment Clause could ensure firstly, that underwear is utilized and secondly, that it is sensible, such as knee length bloomers and a cotton vest.

Finally, the Deed could grant her a licence to attend the wedding that could be withdrawn and have her labelled a trespasser if she ignored her legal obligations. As a trespasser, your sister could be removed from the wedding using reasonable force. In the event of any resistance on the part of your sister, call the police immediately (as if you did not have enough to do).

The removal of your sister from the wedding in handcuffs with appropriate use of a Taser (<u>only</u> if necessary), could be distressing for some of the guests. However, your restraint in the use of a Deed rather than an outright ban would demonstrate that you at least, were prepared to turn the other cheek.

*Thought to be from Kate Middleton regarding her sister Pippa just before her marriage to William.

This is just one of the many complaints received from brides about the conduct of their bridesmaids.

CONCLUSION

I would like to express my gratitude to the many characters in the legal profession and for the strange goings on that I have observed over the years which have made this book possible.

All the best,

Paul Brennan

Sunshine Coast, Queensland

December 2015

John Fytit

John Fytit is the name of the central cartoon character in Law & Disorder cartoons that started in Hong Kong in 1992. He was from the fictitious Hong Kong firm Fytit & Loos (pronounced "Fight it and Lose"). A very unsuccessful name as people read "Fytit" as "Fit it". His International Problem Page started in 2005 and was merged into the *101 Reasons To Kill All the Lawyers* blog.

Paul Brennan

Paul Brennan was born in London. He has worked in the law in various countries including the UK, Canada, Hong Kong and Australia.

He has drawn legal cartoons for the Australian Financial Review, the Hong Kong Tatler and other publications from time to time.

In creating the *101 Reasons To Kill All the Lawyers* blog he explained, "I decided on 101 reasons as I didn't want to depress the entire legal profession by having 1,001."

He is in practice with his wife Diane on Queensland's Sunshine Coast. They have four children.

Other books by the author go to:

http://www.amazon.com/Paul-Brennan/e/B001KMQFEC

 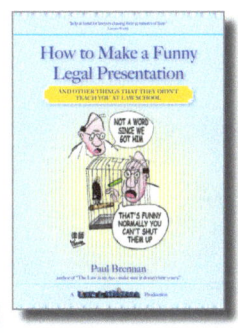 

CONTACT US ON
(07) 5438 8199 or
email: info@lawanddisorder.com.au

SPONSORED by
www.brennanlaw.com.au

www.ingramcontent.com/pod-product-compliance
Lightning Source LLC
Chambersburg PA
CBHW040056100426
42734CB00035B/76